Contents

The First
Palm Sunday

It was the week before the great feast of Passover. Jews from far-off lands travelled to Jerusalem for the celebrations, which lasted several days. Jewish holy men such as the chief priests and Pharisees were waiting to see if Jesus would dare visit the city too. They had been plotting for a long time to arrest and execute the preacher who they

The First
Easter
and other Bible Stories

Retold by Vic Parker

Miles Kelly

First published in 2011 by Miles Kelly Publishing Ltd
Harding's Barn, Bardfield End Green, Thaxted, Essex, CM6 3PX, UK

2 4 6 8 10 9 7 5 3 1

EDITORIAL DIRECTOR *Belinda Gallagher*
ART DIRECTOR *Jo Cowan*
EDITOR *Carly Blake*
DESIGNERS *Michelle Cannatella, Joe Jones*
JUNIOR DESIGNER *Kayleigh Allen*
COVER DESIGNER *Joe Jones*
CONSULTANT *Janet Dyson*
PRODUCTION MANAGER *Elizabeth Collins*
REPROGRAPHICS *Stephan Davis, Ian Paulyn*

ISBN 978-1-84810-402-0

Printed in China

British Library Cataloguing-in-Publication Data
A catalogue record for this book is available from the British Library

ACKNOWLEDGEMENTS
The publishers would like to thank the following artists
who have contributed to this book:

The Bright Agency Katriona Chapman, Dan Crisp,
Giuliano Ferri, Mélanie Florian (inc. cover)
Advocate Art Alida Massari

*The publishers would like to thank Robert Willoughby and
the London School of Theology for their help in compiling this book.*

Made with paper from a sustainable forest

www.mileskelly.net   info@mileskelly.net

www.factsforprojects.com

Self-publish your
children's book

buddingpress.co.uk

thought was stirring up the people and leading them astray. The Jewish leaders thought Jesus might enter Jerusalem unnoticed by mingling among the crowds, so they sent spies through the city to see if they could spot Him.

However Jesus was planning to arrive quite openly. When He and His disciples were a little way off, on the Mount of Olives, Jesus sent two of His friends into the village of Bethphage to find a donkey for Him to ride. "You will find one tethered to a doorway," He told them. "Untie it and bring it to me. If anyone objects, just explain that it's me who needs it and they won't stop you."

The disciples found the donkey, just as He had said. When the owners heard who

wanted it, they brought it to Jesus themselves. They even threw their cloaks onto the donkey's back to make a comfortable saddle for Him to sit on. The little animal had never been ridden before, but it stood calm and willing as Jesus climbed onto it.

Jesus patted the donkey's head, then set off for the city of Jerusalem, with his disciples on foot. When people along the way saw Him coming, they cheered, sang and danced for joy. The ancient prophets had said that the Messiah would ride into Jerusalem on a donkey. And so the people realized that Jesus was claiming openly for the first time that He was the saviour they had been waiting for. "Hosanna!" they shouted, lining the donkey's path with their

cloaks and palm leaves. "Blessed is He who comes in the name of the Lord! Hosanna in the highest!"

People jammed the streets to welcome Jesus all the way into Jerusalem.

"This is outrageous!" the furious Pharisees bellowed at Jesus. "You're making these people think you're the Messiah!"

"Even if they were quiet," Jesus replied, "the stones themselves would cry out to greet me."

Matthew chapter 21; Mark chapter 11; Luke chapter 19; John chapters 11, 12

7

Jesus and the Temple Traders

As all good Jews did at the feast of Passover, Jesus went to pray at the great temple. He expected to see the courtyards filled with respectful worshippers deep in prayer, moving quietly about so as not to disturb others. Instead, Jesus was horrified to find the sacred building being used as a market-place.

Everywhere He looked, there were stallholders selling doves and other animals for sacrifices. They cried out their wares, competing for business. People bartered with them, trying to get the best prices, while doves cooed and lambs bleated. Among the stalls were money-changers, haggling with worshippers and counting out foreign money into Jewish shekels. All the traders were charging unfair prices, and the worshippers had no choice but to pay. Everyone had to offer a sacrifice and give shekels to the temple funds at Passover. Meanwhile, city traders were using the temple courtyards and corridors to get from one side of Jerusalem to another.

As Jesus stood amid the hubbub, he grew more and more furious. Suddenly, He began sending the traders' tables flying into the air, kicking down stalls, smashing dove cages open and ripping animal tethers loose. "This is the house of God, but you have turned it into a robbers' den!" He yelled, clearing the temple of everyone except for genuine worshippers.

It wasn't long before the courtyards were full again. This time, with people who had come to hear Jesus preach.

Matthew chapter 21; Luke chapter 19

10

The Last Supper

The Jewish leaders were extremely frustrated at their failure to get rid of Jesus. One night they gathered at the house of the chief priest, Caiaphas, for an emergency meeting. They were in the middle of discussing what they could do next when there was a knock at the door. A servant ushered in a most unexpected guest. It was Judas Iscariot, one of Jesus' twelve disciples and closest friends.

"I'm here because I can give you what you want," he said, his eyes glinting coldly. "Jesus of Nazareth – how much is He worth to you?"

The Jewish officials didn't know what had made Judas become a traitor – and they didn't care either. They could hardly believe their good luck. They put their heads together for a few moments and then announced, "Thirty pieces of silver."

Without a word, Judas held out his hand and Caiaphas counted out the coins.

From then on, Judas stayed by Jesus' side, waiting for the opportunity to betray Him.

Mysteriously, Jesus knew everything. With a heavy heart, He prepared for one

last meal with His disciples – the Passover supper. He organized a room in secret, so that the Jewish leaders would not find out where He was, and only told His twelve friends about it at the last minute.

The disciples were in a very serious mood as they gathered together. After all, Jesus had warned them two days earlier that He was about to fall into the hands of His enemies and be put to death. As everything Jesus said came true, they were extremely worried.

While they settled at the table, Jesus wrapped a towel around his waist and filled a bowl with water. The disciples were shocked to realize He was going to wash the dust from their feet – a job usually done by the very lowliest servant. Peter was especially shocked and tried to stop Jesus kneeling before Him, but Jesus insisted. "I am setting you all an example," Jesus said afterwards. "Always put others before yourself."

Then it was time for dinner. Jesus took a loaf of bread and asked for God's blessing over it. "This is my body," He said with great sadness, "which will be given up for you." He broke the bread and gave it to all the disciples to eat. Then Jesus poured a cup of wine and asked for God's blessing over that too. "This is my blood," He announced gravely, "the sign of a new promise from God. My blood will be spilt so that everyone's sins will be forgiven." One by one, the disciples took the cup and drank.

Then Jesus gestured for everyone to begin sharing out the different dishes on the table. As they did so, He gave a deep sigh. "I know that one of you will betray me," He said softly. Cries of protest came up from around the table, but Jesus refused to explain further. As the disciples reluctantly turned back to eating, Peter murmured to John, who was sitting closest to Jesus, "Ask Him which of us He means."

John leaned over and spoke in Jesus' ear.

He whispered back, "The one to whom I will give this piece of bread."

John told Peter, and they watched as Jesus tore some bread and offered it to Judas Iscariot. "Do whatever you have to," Jesus told His disloyal friend, "but do it quickly."

And without a word Judas got up from the table and left the room.

Matthew chapter 26; Mark chapter 14; Luke chapter 22; John chapter 13

The Garden of Gethsemane

After Jesus had shared His last supper with the disciples, He sat back and looked around at His dear friends. "I give you a new commandment," He said. "Love each other as I have loved you. By doing this, everyone will know that you are my followers."

"Lord, you've been talking all night as if

you're leaving us," Peter protested.

"Yes," Jesus said gently. "I am going away, and where I am going you won't be able to follow me – for a while, at least."

"Why can't I follow you now?" Peter cried out. "I am ready to die for you!"

But Jesus smiled sadly. "Are you really, my friend?" He asked. "By the time this night is out and the cock has crowed three times at dawn, you will have denied three times that you even know me."

"Never," Peter said, choking with sorrow. "Never." And all the disciples agreed strongly.

"Don't be upset," Jesus tried to comfort them. "I am going to prepare a place for you in my Father's house. And I will return to you for a short while, before I have to go

away again for good. Even then when you will no longer be able to see me, I will always live in your hearts. Later, when the time is right, you will follow and we will be together again. Until then, do what I have done tonight as a way of remembering me. Be at peace, and be happy for me that I am going to be with my Father."

Jesus looked around at His friends' gloomy faces.

"Now come," He said gently. "Let's go to the Mount of Olives. I would like to pray in the Garden of Gethsemane for a while."

As they walked through the moonlight together, Jesus gave the disciples many more important instructions. He knew He only had a short time left in which to talk to them. When they finally reached the

entrance to the Garden of Gethsemane, Jesus saw that the anxious men were exhausted. "Rest here while I go and pray," He told most of them. But He turned to Peter, James and John and said, "I know you are tired, but would you come along with me?"

The three were only too pleased to keep Jesus company. They had never seen Him look so strained and troubled before.

"My heart feels like it's breaking," Jesus sighed heavily when they had gone a little way. "Will you stay while I pray?"

Peter, James and John watched as Jesus sank to his knees, His head in His hands.

"Father!" He cried silently. Jesus prayed that perhaps He might not have to face the suffering He knew lay ahead.

After a long while, Jesus
turned to Peter, James and
John but saw they had
fallen asleep.

So Jesus prayed again. He
felt the sins of all the world
weighing on His shoulders and
He knew the full horror of
what was to come.

Once more Jesus turned
to his friends, but they were
still asleep.

And Jesus prayed again, willingly
accepting the suffering He had to face, so
that all people could one day reach God.

At last Jesus finished praying. Peter, James
and John were still asleep. But at that
moment Judas Iscariot arrived,

accompanied by a band of guards. At the noise of guards' swords and chains and the light from their flaming torches, the disciples woke up, startled.

"Master," Judas said calmly, greeting Jesus with his usual kiss.

At that pre-arranged sign, the guards grabbed Jesus. After a brief commotion and panic, the disciples fled for their lives into the darkness.

Matthew chapter 26; Mark chapter 14; Luke chapter 22; John chapters 13, 14, 18

Jesus on Trial

That night Jesus was marched into the city of Jerusalem, to the great house of the high priest, Caiaphas. Inside Caiaphas' mansion, Jesus was quizzed by Annas, the former high priest. What did He think about ancient holy writings? What miracles did He claim to have worked? Who did He think He was?

Jesus refused to answer and was marched to a room full of Jewish officials. They had witnesses who they had paid to lie, accusing Jesus of saying and doing things that were against Jewish law. But the witnesses couldn't get their stories straight!

Finally Caiaphas hissed, "I order you to tell us, under solemn oath, whether you think you are the Son of God."

"I am," He said with grace, "and one day you will see the Son of Man seated at the right hand of the Father in Heaven."

"Blasphemy!" roared Caiaphas, a satisfied gleam in his eyes. Blasphemy was the crime of lying against God for which the punishment was death.

In triumph, the Jewish elders had Jesus blindfolded. They slapped and kicked Him,

shouting, "Prophesy for us now, Messiah. Guess who hit you!" And in the morning, they had Jesus brought in front of the Roman governor, Pontius Pilate. Only he could approve an execution.

The news spread around the city and an enormous crowd gathered outside.

Pilate asked Jesus many more questions. Are you really a king? Have you been plotting against the Roman government? Have you been planning a rebellion?

Perplexed, Pilate couldn't find that Jesus had done anything wrong. He ordered that Jesus also be questioned by Herod, the ruler of Galilee, who was in Jerusalem at that time. But Herod couldn't find Jesus guilty of anything either. Even Pilate's wife told him that she had had a dream in which Jesus of

Nazareth was innocent of all charges. "Have nothing further to do with him," she advised her husband.

Pilate made his decision. He went out onto the balcony of his judgement hall and announced to the waiting crowds, "This man has done nothing to deserve death. He shall be whipped and let go." And Jesus was dragged off for His punishment.

Meanwhile the Jewish officials had

mingled with the crowds, persuading them that Jesus was guilty of blasphemy. As Pilate turned to go back into his Judgement Hall, people sent up cries of, "Kill him! Kill Jesus of Nazareth!"

But the Roman governor was deeply disturbed, he did not know what for.

Suddenly he had an idea. Pilate remembered that it was Passover and there was a custom for the governor to release one prisoner of the people's choice. In the cells was a murderer called Barabbas. Pilate felt sure that the people would rather have Jesus released than a violent killer.

"Who shall I pardon – Barabbas or Jesus of Nazareth?" Pilate asked the crowd.

He couldn't believe his ears when the shouts came back, "Barabbas!"

Pilate ordered that Jesus be brought in front of him once more. He had been whipped until blood poured down His back. The guards had mocked Jesus as the King of the Jews, too, by pressing a crown of thorns onto His head and throwing a cloak around His shoulders.

Now the crowd jeered too.

Pilate had had enough. He called for water and a towel, and washed his hands in front of everyone. "I cleanse myself of this man's blood," he announced.

Then Barabbas was released and Jesus was led away to be crucified.

Matthew chapters 26, 27; Mark chapters 14, 15;
Luke chapters 22, 23; John chapters 18, 19

The Crucifixion

Jesus had withstood being marched about in chains, hours of angry questioning, a beating from the Jewish officials, and being brutally whipped by Pilate's guards. The crown of thorns was still pressed into His head, sending blood trickling down His pained-filled face.

Two Roman soldiers lifted a huge, solid

wooden cross over Jesus' shoulder – so heavy that He nearly collapsed from the weight of it. Then Jesus staggered onwards, through the streets of Jerusalem and towards the hill outside the city where He and two other criminals were to be executed.

Thousands of people lined the way, watching the procession. Jesus willed Himself forwards, heavy step after heavy step. But eventually He crashed into the dust, utterly exhausted. The angry guards dragged a strong man from the crowd called Simon of Cyrene and ordered him to carry the cross instead.

People in the crowd yelled insults and spat on Jesus as He stumbled by. But Jesus caught sight of the sorrowful faces of many friends He had made too. Many of the women were weeping. "Don't cry for me," Jesus said, "but for yourselves, your children and for the destruction that is to come."

Eventually they reached the place for the execution. It was called Golgotha, meaning 'place of the skull'. A soldier made Jesus lie down on the cross, and long nails were hammered into His hands and feet. "Father forgive them, for they don't know what they are doing," Jesus moaned. A notice was fixed above his head which said 'Jesus of Nazareth, King of the Jews' in three languages. "It shouldn't say that," some Jewish officials objected. "It should say 'This man said he was the King of the Jews'."

But the Roman governor, Pilate, boomed, "I ordered it to be written just like that and that is the way it will stay!"

The Jewish officials mocked as Jesus' cross was hoisted up high. "You said you're the Son of God – so save yourself!"

As the two criminals were raised on crosses either side of Jesus, one sneered, "Yes, save yourself and save us too!"

"How dare you!" the second thief groaned. "We deserve this, but Jesus is innocent. Lord, remember me when you reach your kingdom."

"I promise you," whispered Jesus, "today you will be with me in paradise."

Even though it was midday, darkness suddenly fell over the land. Close by at the foot of the cross, was Jesus' heartbroken mother, and His close friends including John, Mary Magdalene and Salome.

"Mother, take care of John as if he were your own son," Jesus murmered. "John, look after my mother as if she were your own."

Jesus hung in agony on the cross for three long hours. Then He lifted His head and cried aloud, "My God! Why have you abandoned me?" Somebody rushed to lift a stick with a sponge on the end that had been dipped in wine so He could have a drink. Jesus cried out again, "Father, I give up my spirit into your hands. It is finished." And His head drooped.

At that very moment, the earth rumbled

and shook, and rocks split open. People said that the great curtain in the temple ripped from top to bottom. Others said they saw graves open and spirits rise from them.

A Roman officer at the foot of the cross looked up and gasped, "This man truly was the Son of God."

Matthew chapter 27; Mark chapter 15; Luke chapter 23; John chapter 19

The First Easter

The evening after Jesus had been put to death, a wealthy Jew called Joseph of Arimathea begged Pontius Pilate to allow him to bury Jesus' body. Pilate agreed. So Joseph went with his friend, Nicodemus, back to Golgotha, where women were still weeping at the foot of His cross. Gently, Joseph and Nicodemus lifted Jesus' poor, bleeding body down. They wrapped Him in a linen shroud with burial spices and, accompanied by the sobbing women, took Him to a nearby cemetery. There the two men laid Jesus in a small, cave-like tomb that Joseph had already paid for, and rolled a heavy stone across the entrance. Full of grief and with nothing else to do, they left.

Meanwhile, some Jewish officials had been to see Pilate. "Jesus of Nazareth said He would rise up again after three days," they told the Roman governor. "Have soldiers guard His tomb so no one can steal the body, then tell everyone that He's miraculously come back to life." Pilate nodded and sent the men away.

Pilate's guards sat outside Jesus' tomb through the night of that first Good Friday

– nothing happened. They kept watch all the next day and again nobody came. But as dawn broke on the Sabbath, the third day, the earth suddenly shook so violently that it knocked the soldiers off their feet. A white light blazed out of the sky and shone over the tomb. Through the glare, the terrified soldiers watched the glowing figure of a man roll away the massive stone from the tomb entrance. The soldiers were scared by what they saw and fled for their lives.

Not long afterwards a group of grieving women arrived at the cemetery to pay their respects at the tomb. They included Jesus' friends Mary Magdalene, Mary the mother of James and John, Salome and Joanna. When they saw that the soldiers were gone and the stone had been rolled away, they

screamed in horror. Someone must have stolen Jesus' body!

Inside the tomb where Jesus' body should have been, two shining men were sitting.

"Why are you looking for the living among the dead?" the men said.

"Don't you remember that the Son of Man said He would rise on the third day?"

Mary Magdalene raced to fetch the disciples Peter and John. When the two men saw the empty tomb they were full of anger. They went off to try to find out who had taken the body. Mary sank down

outside the tomb, sobbing. Then suddenly she sensed someone behind her. Mary span around and through her tears she saw a blurry figure whom she thought must be the cemetery gardener. "Why are you weeping?" the man asked.

"If you moved the body," she begged, "please tell me where to."

The man said just one word.

"Mary."

Mary's heart stood still. Suddenly, she recognized the man – it was Jesus!

"Go now," Jesus said softly, as Mary fell at His feet, gazing up at Him in wonder. "Find the disciples and tell them that I will soon be returning to my Father."

Meanwhile, the other women who had seen the empty tomb were hurrying

homewards when all at once, a man appeared out of nowhere on the road in front of them. "Good morning," He said.

The women were amazed and couldn't believe who they were hearing and seeing.

"Don't be afraid," Jesus said. "Go and tell my disciples to travel to Galilee and I will meet them there soon."

Matthew chapters 27, 28; Mark chapter 16; Luke chapters 23, 24; John chapters 19, 20